CONTEMPLATING

LIFE'S GREATEST QUESTIONS

Would you be so kind as to return this book to

Lena Scallion

CONTEMPLATING
LIFE'S GREATEST QUESTIONS

Selections from the

Writings of

Bahá'u'lláh

with Commentary

Edited by M.K. Rohani

Contemplating Life's Greatest Questions
by M.K. Rohani

Oneworld Publications Ltd
185 Banbury Road, Oxford, OX2 7AR

© Oneworld Publications Ltd 1991
All rights reserved. Copyright under Berne Convention
A CIP record for this book is available from the British Library

ISBN 1-85168-024-1

Printed in Great Britain by
The Guernsey Press Co. Ltd., Guernsey, Channel Islands.

*'Do not question too much,
lest your head fall off.'*
Brihad-aranyaka Upanishad 3:6

contents

Introduction

9

How did the universe come into existence?

14

Does God exist?

27

What is the purpose of life?

46

Why is there suffering and evil in the world?

58

Is there life after death?

71

Conclusion

90

Bibliography

94

INTRODUCTION

The fourth-century Greek philosopher Socrates once said that the unexamined life is not a life worth living. He was obviously a man deeply interested in life's questions. For him, life's meaning and attraction lay in solving its questions and unravelling its secrets. Perhaps Socrates was very confident about his ability to discover answers. Others have been less optimistic. In 1897, the French symbolist painter Paul Gauguin, troubled by life's difficulties and the unanswerable mysteries, was inspired to paint a large painting which he entitled, 'Where do we come from, where are we going'. Afterwards he took arsenic in an attempt to commit suicide. The attempt failed and he at last resigned himself to living with both his difficulties and life's mysteries. Of course, these men were not alone in their curiosity and anxieties. The questions of life have given birth to many systems of philosophy, various branches of science, and even more numerous schools of religious thought. All of these testify to the many different ways of approaching the mysteries of existence.

Despite the difficulty of solving life's mysteries or finding a way to live with them, it is impossible to imagine that the pursuit of answers to these questions will ever be abandoned. The enduring nature of this quest is ensured by the fact that how we perceive these mysteries shapes every aspect of human activity and thought. Questions such as: Is there a God?, Is there life after death?, Is there a purpose to life?, Do people have souls?, affect our concept of justice, our beliefs about the sanctity of life, morality, and so on, and these beliefs and concepts effect everything. They shape our views about criminal justice, abortion, community responsibility, the use of violence, even whether or not we pay taxes or choose to get out of bed in the morning to go to work.

In this book, *Life's Greatest Questions*, we will examine one of the recent sources of knowledge about these questions, the teachings of Bahá'u'lláh, the nineteenth century Prophet-Founder of the Bahá'í Faith. Bahá'u'lláh belongs, especially in His use of language and terminology, to the Western religious tradition. Nevertheless, His vision is not limited to one region of the world; the most dominating characteristic or theme of His message is its world-embracing vision. Many of Bahá'u'lláh's spiritual teachings are centred on the precept that the human race is one. In His teachings the oneness of humankind is presented as a spiritual truth that is vital to the peace and prosperity of all. It encompasses the equality of men and women, the need for an auxiliary world language, the need for universal education, and the necessity and inevitability of a world government. As such, a superficial reading might lead the reader to infer that His writings put more emphasis on ethical and social issues than on answers to metaphysical questions. But, in fact, Bahá'u'lláh's social and ethical teachings are inextricable from metaphysical and spiritual concepts. For example, His teaching of the oneness of humanity is 'God-centred' in that it is based upon the unity and reality of God. It is also based on the teaching that the all-encompassing love of God for humankind is not and cannot be limited by nationalism, racism or cultural prejudice. In order for us to draw close to God we must share in His love for all people. All of Bahá'u'lláh's teachings and the answers He provides to the eternal questions of life lead back to the attributes of God and the ethical fundamentals of the spiritual life.

Truth, as He saw it, centres in a way of life based on a relationship to God, vital, inescapable, and too valuable to be compromised. His teachings were considered radical in nineteenth-century Persia (Iran). Not surprisingly, they provoked the hostility of the orthodox and conservative. Similarly, the devotion He inspired in so many admirers inflamed the envy and jealousy of many who were hungry for leadership. Consequently, He spent most of His life as a prisoner and an exile. Yet He willingly bore these hardships in the belief that what He had to offer the world necessitated such a level of sacrifice.

When He spoke about the authority of His teachings, He frequently stated that this authority was vested in the teachings themselves, in their own intrinsic spiritual value, and not solely on His claim to revealed truth. In other words, if we lived by them we would come to know their value. No other proof is needed. He openly told His followers not to mention or rely on accounts of miracles.

During His life, Bahá'u'lláh set forth His teachings

in a profusion of books and letters sent to friends, admirers, family members and even to some of the most despotic political and religious leaders of His time. Some of these writings were written in response to questions. It is these responses which provide us with the primary source material for this book.

When considering the answers which Bahá'u'lláh provided, it is important to keep in mind both the narrower cultural context in which He lived and the broader context of His life's mission. This means we have to understand that He used the symbols and religious terminology accepted by the people to whom He was speaking; He even used them in a way that often reflected the recipient's limited understanding. For example, there were times when Bahá'u'lláh used symbols as if they were literal and other times when He acknowledged that reality does not lie in the symbol itself, but what it points to. Bahá'u'lláh's response to the questions seemed to depend on, and be shaped by, the capacity and understanding of those whom He was trying to reach. Thus, we must keep in mind the background of His questioners, their limitations, and the reasons they asked the questions. We also need to examine the relationship between His answers and the spiritual response He sought to evoke.

Some of His answers can clearly be understood and interpreted from a variety of standpoints and on a number of levels, but in every case the answers are intended to impart some spiritual insight. It is this aspect of His answers that transcends the limited cultural context in which He lived and takes us into the broader context of His life's mission. Because Bahá'u'lláh's ultimate concern was the spiritual life, He does not always give us the type of answers we are expecting or seeking. Even when He appears to be answering a question involving material issues, His metaphorical use of language transforms the subject into a spiritual message. He speaks to our religious impulse; the impulse within us which is, in its most sincere sense, a response to life's mysteries, a longing to know the meaning of our existence. It is an impulse that inevitably arises out of the fears, hopes, frustrations and curiosities that are intrinsic to our life. It is also an impulse that encompasses our deepest appreciation of the beauty of life itself.

HOW DID THE UNIVERSE COME INTO EXISTENCE?

Through the ages some philosophers have approached the question of existence from the perspective of how to determine and define what constitutes 'real existence'. In Bahá'u'lláh's writings the term 'existence' is given a specifically theological meaning wherein existence becomes relative to the spiritual condition of the individual. Real existence is therefore equated with spiritual existence. Relative to this real existence, material existence is metaphorically signified as non-existence.

Bahá'u'lláh's answers are not attempts at an objective scientific analysis of the origin of material phenomena or a presentation of tangible evidence to be verified in a laboratory. This approach, too often applied to the spiritual content of sacred literature, is altogether foreign to His aim. Bahá'u'lláh's message is ultimately addressed to the soul of the individual, and is intended to evoke a spiritual response and awareness in the heart of the questioner beyond the simple presentation of 'facts'. Only the experience of the individual can substantiate His assertions.

There are perhaps three specific spiritual contexts in which Bahá'u'lláh speaks of existence:

The beginning of creation as a symbol for the birth of personal spiritual awareness.

The value of spiritual existence in relation to material existence.

The nature of God as revealed metaphorically and symbolically in material existence.

Concerning the beginning or act of creation as a symbol for the birth of personal spiritual awareness, He writes, 'In every age and cycle He [God] hath, through the splendorous light shed by the Manifestations of His wondrous Essence*, recreated all things, so that whatsoever reflecteth in the heavens and on the earth the signs of His glory may not be deprived of the outpourings of His mercy, nor despair of the showers of His favours' (*Gleanings* 61). In the same connection He states, 'Such as communicate the generating influence and such as receive its impact are indeed created through the irresistible Word of God which is the Cause of the entire creation, while all else besides His Word are but the creatures and the effects thereof' (*Tablets of Bahá'u'lláh* 140). The whole idea of creation is, for

---

* By 'Manifestations of His wondrous Essence' Bahá'u'lláh means individuals such as Moses, Jesus Christ, Muhammad, the Buddha and others whose lives reflected the nature of God and who imparted spiritual enlightenment to the people around them.

Bahá'u'lláh, an existence based on and originating from the mystical 'Word'. These statements suggest that the scriptural portrait of the original act of bringing the universe into being can be understood as a metaphor for the creation of faith and spirituality in the individual.

Concerning the value of spiritual existence in relation to material existence, this is exemplified by the individuals He speaks of who were so caught up in 'their yearning for God' and 'transports of ecstatic delight' that 'the world and all that is therein faded before their eyes into nothingness' (*Kitáb-i-Iqán* 156). This emphasis on spiritual existence is further reflected in many passages where He urges detachment from the world. He writes, 'It is incumbent upon thee . . . to cleanse the eye of thine heart from the things of the world, that thou mayest realize the infinitude of divine knowledge, and mayest behold Truth so clearly that thou wilt need no proof to demonstrate His reality, nor any evidence to bear witness unto His testimony' (ibid. 91). These statements clearly show that Bahá'u'lláh places spiritual existence before material existence in importance. It is not surprising therefore that He addresses the issue of the origin of existence as a mean of conveying spiritual insights rather than as a scientific account of the origin of material phenomena.

With regard to the metaphorical relationship between creation and God, Bahá'u'lláh writes:

> whatever is in the heavens and whatever is on the earth is a direct evidence of the revelation within it of the attributes and names of God, inasmuch as

within every atom are enshrined the signs that bear eloquent testimony to the revelation of that most great Light. (*Kitáb-i-Iqán* 100)

Direct knowledge of the actual creation of the universe is beyond the realm of any individual's experiential knowledge, but Bahá'u'lláh uses the idea of a created universe and the characteristics of material existence metaphorically, irrespective of verifiable proof, to set forth an understanding of God.

When Bahá'u'lláh addresses the question of the origin of creation more directly He relates it to the attributes of God. For example, He states that for God to be the creator of the universe there would always have to have been a creation. For if we imagine that there was a time when the creation did not exist, then there would be a time when God had not yet become the creator and this contradicts the eternal nature of God. He writes:

> The one true God hath everlastingly existed, and will everlastingly continue to exist. His creation, likewise, hath had no beginning, and will have no end. All that is created, however, is preceded by a cause. This fact, in itself, establisheth, beyond the shadow of a doubt, the unity of the Creator. (*Gleanings* 162)

The nature of God transcends the limitations inherent in the realm of place and time. Thus God cannot be conceived of in a chronological context such as existing before creation. Logically, therefore, if we are to understand the origins of material creation, we must accept that if God exists, material creation has also always existed and is renewed rather than born. This process of renewal is in fact intrinsic to the contingent nature of material creation, distinguishing it from the eternal, changeless nature of God. The answer to the mystery of creation cannot be separated from the mystery of God.

The key to understanding Bahá'u'lláh's answers is recognizing that they only touch on the actual questions about creation in so far as they evoke spiritual insights and experiences. This is particularly evident when He suggests that references in sacred literature to the beginning of creation are symbolic of the awakening of humanity's spiritual awareness. The actual temporal beginning of material phenomena, something beyond personal verification, is not the central point. Instead, Bahá'u'lláh brings us in touch with this mystery through spiritual truth verifiable in our own experience. The overall message is that people who live for the world alone are non-existent and in need of being recreated into a spiritual existence. They are brought into this spiritual existence through a twofold process of becoming aware of their spiritual reality and being detached from the contingent world. This awakening of the individual's spiritual life is set forth by Bahá'u'lláh as the very reason for which creation has been called into being.

*Excerpts from
the
Writings of Bahá'u'lláh*

✣

As regards thine assertions about the beginning of creation, this is a matter on which conceptions vary by reason of the divergences in men's thoughts and opinions. Wert thou to assert that it hath ever existed and shall continue to exist, it would be true; or wert thou to affirm the same concept as is mentioned in the sacred Scriptures, no doubt would there be about it, for it hath been revealed by God, the Lord of the worlds. Indeed He was a hidden treasure. This is a station that can never be described nor even alluded to. And in the station of 'I did wish to make Myself known', God was, and His creation had ever existed beneath His shelter from the beginning that hath no beginning, apart from its being preceded by a Firstness which cannot be regarded as firstness and originated by a Cause inscrutable even unto all men of learning.

That which hath been in existence had existed before, but not in the form thou seest today. The world of existence came into being through the heat generated from the interaction between the active force and that which is its recipient. These two are the same, yet they are different. Thus doth the Great Announcement inform thee about this glorious structure. Such as communicate the generating influence and such as receive its impact are indeed created through the irresistible Word of God which is the Cause of the entire creation, while all else besides His Word are but the creatures and the effects thereof. Verily thy Lord is the Expounder, the All-Wise.

Know thou, moreover, that the Word of God - exalted be His glory - is higher and far superior to that which the senses can perceive, for it is sanctified from any property or substance. It transcendeth the limitations of known elements and is exalted above all the essential and recognized substances. It became manifest without any syllable or sound and is none but the Command of God which pervadeth all created things. It hath never been withheld from the world of being. It is God's all-pervasive grace, from which all grace doth emanate. It is an entity far removed above all that hath been and shall be. (*Tablets of Bahá'u'lláh* 140-1)

As to thy question concerning the origin of creation. Know assuredly that God's creation hath existed from eternity, and will continue to exist forever. Its beginning hath had no beginning, and its end knoweth no end. His name, the Creator, presupposeth a creation, even as His title, the Lord of Men, must involve the existence of a servant.

As to those sayings, attributed to the Prophets of old, such as, 'In the beginning was God; there was no creature to know Him', and 'The Lord was alone; with no one to adore Him', the meaning of these and similar sayings is clear and evident, and should at no time be misapprehended. To this same truth bear witness these words which He hath revealed: 'God was alone; there was none else besides Him. He will always remain what He hath ever been.' Every discerning eye will readily perceive that the Lord is now manifest, yet there is none to recognize His glory. By this is meant that the habitation wherein the Divine Being dwelleth is far above the reach and ken of any one besides Him. Whatsoever in the contingent world can either be expressed or apprehended, can never transgress the limits which, by its inherent nature, have been imposed upon it. God, alone, transcendeth such limitations. He, verily, is from everlasting. No peer or partner has been, or can ever be, joined with Him. No name can be compared with His Name. No pen can portray His nature, neither can any tongue depict His glory. He will, for ever, remain immeasurably exalted above any one except Himself.

Consider the hour at which the supreme Manifestation of God revealeth Himself unto men. Ere that hour cometh, the Ancient Being, Who is still unknown of men and hath not as yet given utterance to the Word of God, is Himself the All-Knower in a world devoid of any man that hath known Him. He is indeed the Creator without a creation. For at the very moment preceding His Revelation, each and every created thing shall be made to yield up its soul to God. This is indeed the Day of which it hath been written: 'Whose shall be the Kingdom this Day?' And none can be found ready to answer! (*Gleanings* 151-2)

And now, concerning thy question regarding the creation of man. Know thou that all men have been created in the nature made by God, the Guardian, the Self-Subsisting. Unto each one hath been prescribed a pre-ordained measure, as decreed in God's mighty and guarded Tablets. All that which ye potentially possess can, however, be manifested only as a result of your own volition. Your own acts testify to this truth. Consider, for instance, that which hath been forbidden, in the Bayán, unto men. God hath in that Book, and by His behest, decreed as lawful whatsoever He hath pleased to decree, and hath, through the power of His sovereign might, forbidden whatsoever He elected to forbid. To this testifieth the text of that Book. Will ye not bear witness? Men, however, have wittingly broken His law. Is such a behaviour to be attributed to God, or to their proper selves? Be fair in your judgement. Every good thing is of God, and every evil thing is from yourselves.

Will ye not comprehend? This same truth hath been revealed in all the Scriptures, if ye be of them that understand. (*Gleanings* 149)

⚙

As to thy question concerning the worlds of God. Know thou of a truth that the worlds of God are countless in their number, and infinite in their range. None can reckon or comprehend them except God, the All-Knowing, the All-Wise. Consider thy state when asleep. Verily, I say, this phenomenon is the most mysterious of the signs of God amongst men, were they to ponder it in their hearts. Behold how the thing which thou hast seen in thy dream is, after a considerable lapse of time, fully realized. Had the world in which thou didst find thyself in thy dream been identical with the world in which thou livest, it would have been necessary for the event occurring in that dream to have transpired in this world at the very moment of its occurrence. Were it so, you yourself would have borne witness unto it. This being not the case, however, it must necessarily follow that the world in which thou livest is different and apart from that which thou hast experienced in thy dream. This latter world hath neither beginning nor end. It would be true if thou wert to contend that this same world is, as decreed by the All-Glorious and Almighty God, within thy proper self and is wrapped up within thee. It would equally be true to maintain that thy spirit, having transcended the limitations of sleep and having stripped itself of all earthly attachment, hath, by the act of God, been made to traverse a realm which lieth hidden in the innermost reality of this world. Verily I say, the creation of God embraceth worlds besides this world, and creatures apart from these creatures. In each of these worlds He hath ordained things which none can search except Himself, the All-Searching, the All-Wise. Do thou meditate on that which We have revealed unto thee, that thou mayest discover the purpose of God, thy Lord, and the Lord of all worlds. In these words the mysteries of Divine Wisdom have been treasured. We have refrained from dwelling upon this theme owing to the sorrow that hath encompassed Us from the actions of them that have been created through Our words, if ye be of them that will hearken unto Our Voice. (*Gleanings* 152-3)

✣

Every thing must needs have an origin and every building a builder. Verily, the Word of God is the Cause which hath preceded the contingent world - a world which is adorned with the splendours of the Ancient of Days, yet is being renewed and regenerated at all times. Immeasurably exalted is the God of Wisdom Who hath raised this sublime structure.

Look at the world and ponder a while upon it. It unveileth the book of its own self before thine eyes and revealeth that which the Pen of thy Lord, the Fashioner, the All-Informed, hath inscribed therein. It will acquaint thee with that which is within it and upon it and will give thee such clear explanations as to make thee independent of every eloquent expounder.

Say: Nature in its essence is the embodiment of My Name, the Maker, the Creator. Its manifestations are diversified by varying causes, and in this diversity there are signs for men of discernment. Nature is God's Will and is its expression in and through the contingent world. It is a dispensation of Providence ordained by the Ordainer, the All-Wise. Were anyone to affirm that it is the Will of God as manifested in the world of being, no one should question this assertion. It is endowed with a power whose reality men of learning fail to grasp. Indeed a man of insight can perceive naught therein save the effulgent splendour of Our Name, the Creator. Say: This is an existence which knoweth no decay, and Nature itself is lost in bewilderment before its revelations, its compelling evidences and its effulgent glory which have encompassed the universe.

It ill beseemeth thee to turn thy gaze unto former or more recent times. Make thou mention of this Day and magnify that which hath appeared therein. It will in truth suffice all mankind. Indeed expositions and discourses in explanation of such things cause the spirits to be chilled. It behoveth thee to speak forth in such wise as to set the hearts of true believers ablaze and cause their bodies to soar.

Whoso firmly believeth today in the rebirth of man and is fully conscious that God, the Most Exalted, wieldeth supreme ascendancy and absolute authority over this new creation, verily such a man is reckoned with them that are endued with insight in this most great Revelation. Unto this beareth witness every discerning believer. (*Tablets of Bahá'u'lláh* 141-2)

DOES GOD EXIST?

The question of whether there is a God cannot be answered without first considering and determining what is meant by 'God'. However, 'God' is perhaps the most elusive of all mysteries to define. If we consider the many definitions or concepts of God that exist, it is perhaps not stretching things too far to say that God has come to be understood or defined as the *answer* behind all the mysteries of life encountered in the human experience. One such example would be the question of the universe's origin, where God has traditionally been understood as the creative force underlying the beginning of all things.

It has long been recognized that there is a fundamental logic suggesting a cause underlying anything that has come into existence. As Plato said, 'That which is created must, as we affirm, of necessity be created by a cause. But the father and maker of all this universe is past finding out' (*Timaeus* 28). Or, in the words of Augustine, 'though the voices of the prophets were silent, the world itself, by its well-ordered changes and movements and by the fair appearance of all visible things, bears a testimony of its own, both that it has been created and also that it could not have been created save by God, whose greatness and beauty are unutterable and invisible' (*City of God* XI:4).

This logic has its own limitations and we find ourselves back at the original mystery of how are we to understand the existence of a primal Cause which, as we understand, has itself no cause? If we accept that God is the answer to this and other mysteries it appears that we are simply replacing one mystery with another. This may be so in some senses, but it is also true that, in understanding God as the answer, God becomes more than merely another mystery. God becomes, rather, a focal point putting all the other mysteries of life in the context of our own lives. It becomes an answer around which human life has been organized, perceived, and even preserved as sacred. The concepts of social unity, sacredness, and reverence for life are all bound together with the mystery often spoken of as God.

The understanding of God has taken on many forms in the history of religious thought. However, there is a general evolution in religious understanding whereby the concept of God becomes increasingly less anthropomorphic, that is, represented by limited physical forms, and instead, more exalted and unknowable. While these ideas help provide us with a clearer definition or understanding of God, acknowledging God as the answer to other mysteries still leaves us with the original questions: 'What is the answer to the mystery of God? Is God merely a concept or is God a reality?'

It may be that God is both. If we accept the definition of God as a reality embracing such qualities as eternality, omniscience and omnipresence, then any concept we could formulate would not exhaust the full extent of God's nature and would therefore remain at a purely conceptual level, not entirely rooted in reality. In other words, even if we acknowledge that God exists, with our limited perception it is impossible for us to form an accurate understanding or true comprehension of such a reality.

Bahá'u'lláh does not dwell at length on the traditional arguments or logic offered for substantiating that God is a reality, even though such arguments may be inferred from His overall theological message. Instead His writings seem to stress a more experiential approach to the issue. For Him it is not arguments or abstract answers but spiritual responses and experiences that matter. Bahá'u'lláh's writings state that God reveals Himself in the world of being in many ways and the truth of such revelations of God is something we only come to know in the process of responding to it. Bahá'u'lláh does not attempt to enable people to grasp the reality of God intellectually. God is, in Bahá'u'lláh's words, unknowable. Instead, His message enables us to attain the 'Presence of God'. It is within the experiential contexts of this 'Presence' that we are able to know, and affirm, the existence of God even though we are unable to 'know' God in a direct or full sense.

God can only be known from those things in the realm of creation that show His attributes. This is a religious teaching dating back to ancient times. Paul wrote, 'For since the creation of the world His invisible attributes are clearly seen, being understood by the things that are made, even His eternal power and Godhead' (*Romans* 1:20). Similarly, Bahá'u'lláh points out:

> Manifold are the verses that have been repeatedly revealed in all the heavenly Books and the holy Scriptures, expressive of this most subtle and lofty theme. Even as He hath revealed: 'We will surely show them Our signs in the world and within themselves.' Again He saith: 'And also in your own selves: will ye not then behold the signs of God?' And yet again He revealeth: 'And be ye not like those who forget God, and whom He hath therefore caused to forget their own selves.' In this connection, He Who is the eternal King . . . hath spoken: 'He hath known God who hath known himself' (*Kitáb-i-Iqán* 101-2).

And again He states, 'all things, in their inmost reality, testify to the revelation of the names and attributes of God within them' (ibid. 102).

Although all things proceed from God, Bahá'u'lláh, for the purpose of instruction, appears to distinguish human attributes from divine attributes. He indicates that God is 'exalted beyond every human attribute', that is, those attributes that have inherent limitations owing to their created nature, such as 'corporeal existence, ascent and descent, egress and regress' (ibid. 98). But, while He states that God does not possess human attributes, humanity, on the other hand, is capable of possessing the attributes of God. In fact He says:

> How resplendent the luminaries of knowledge that shine in an atom, and how vast the oceans of wisdom that surge within a drop! To a supreme degree is this true of man, who, among all created things, hath been invested with the robe of such gifts, and hath been singled out for the glory of such distinction. For in him are potentially revealed all the attributes and names of God to a degree that no other created being hath excelled or surpassed. All these names and attributes are applicable to him. Even as He hath said: 'Man is My mystery, and I am his mystery.' (ibid. 101)

Given that these divine attributes are potentially revealed in the human individual, it is possible to say that God is revealed mystically within us. As Bahá'u'lláh says, 'He hath known God who hath known himself' (ibid. 102). Naturally, the degree to which this potential is realized varies according to the capacities and efforts of each person. As He states, 'Each according to its capacity, indicateth, and is expressive of, the knowledge of God' (ibid. 103). However, Bahá'u'lláh states that 'of all men, the most accomplished, the most distinguished and the most excellent are the Manifestations of the Sun of Truth' (ibid. 103). By this phrase, 'the Manifestations of the Sun of Truth', He is referring to individuals such as Jesus Christ, Muhammad, Buddha and others, as well as Himself. These persons, He taught, were like perfectly clear mirrors reflecting the light of God.

Such persons are regarded by Bahá'u'lláh as 'Gems of Holiness' whom 'the Source of infinite grace' (that is, God) has caused to appear 'out of the realm of the spirit' so that they 'may impart unto the world the mysteries of the unchangeable Being, and tell of the subtleties of His imperishable Essence' (ibid. 99). They manifest the attributes of God in the way they lived their lives and in the knowledge they imparted; the evidence of their divinity may also be seen in the long religious traditions they inspired and needs no comment here.

However, there are significant conclusions to be drawn about God just from the connection Bahá'u'lláh makes between the lives of these persons and the existence of God. The fact that Bahá'u'lláh states that God has 'caused' such persons to exist so that God's guidance and reality might be known indicates that He regards God as having an active presence in history, a will, and a love for His creation. Bahá'u'lláh's concept of God is not impersonal but dynamic and immediate. For example, He writes, 'the manifold bounties of the Lord of all beings have, at all times, through the Manifestations of His divine Essence, encompassed the earth and all that dwell therein. Not for a moment hath His grace been withheld, nor have the showers of His loving-kindness ceased to rain upon mankind' (ibid. 14). This a view that permeates all His writings.

Excerpts from
the
Writings of Bahá'u'lláh

✦

We testify that He is One in His Essence, One in His Attributes. He hath none to equal Him in the whole universe, nor any partner in all creation. He hath sent forth His Messengers, and sent down His Books, that they may announce unto His creatures the Straight Path. (*Epistle* 98)

✦

Lauded and glorified art Thou, O Lord, my God! How can I make mention of Thee, assured as I am that no tongue, however deep its wisdom, can befittingly magnify Thy name, nor can the bird of the human heart, however great its longing, ever hope to ascend into the heaven of Thy majesty and knowledge.

If I describe Thee, O my God, as Him Who is the All-

Perceiving, I find myself compelled to admit that They Who are the highest Embodiments of perception have been created by virtue of Thy behest. And if I extol Thee as Him Who is the All-Wise, I, likewise, am forced to recognize that the Well Springs of wisdom have themselves been generated through the operation of Thy Will. And if I proclaim Thee as the Incomparable One, I soon discover that they Who are the inmost essence of oneness have been sent down by Thee and are but the evidences of Thine handiwork. And if I acclaim Thee as the Knower of all things, I must confess that they Who are the Quintessence of knowledge are but the creation and instruments of Thy Purpose.

Exalted, immeasurably exalted, art Thou above the strivings of mortal man to unravel Thy mystery, to describe Thy glory, or even to hint at the nature of Thine Essence. For whatever such strivings may accomplish, they never can hope to transcend the limitations imposed upon Thy creatures, inasmuch as these efforts are actuated by Thy decree, and are begotten of Thine invention. The loftiest sentiments which the holiest of saints can express in praise of Thee, and the deepest wisdom which the most learned of men can utter in their attempts to comprehend Thy nature, all revolve around that Centre Which is wholly subjected to Thy sovereignty, Which adoreth Thy Beauty, and is propelled through the movement of Thy Pen. (*Gleanings* 3-4)

Far, far from Thy glory be what mortal man can affirm of Thee, or attribute unto Thee, or the praise with which he can glorify Thee! Whatever duty Thou hast prescribed unto Thy servants of extolling to the utmost Thy majesty and glory is but a token of Thy grace unto them, that they may be enabled to ascend unto the station conferred upon their own inmost being, the station of the knowledge of their own selves.

No one else besides Thee hath, at any time, been able to fathom Thy mystery, or befittingly to extol Thy greatness. Unsearchable and high above the praise of men wilt Thou remain for ever. There is none other God but Thee, the Inaccessible, the Omnipotent, the Omniscient, the Holy of Holies. (*Gleanings* 4-5)

To every discerning and illuminated heart it is evident that God, the unknowable Essence, the Divine Being, is immensely exalted beyond every human attribute, such as corporeal existence, ascent and descent, egress and regress. Far be it from His glory that human tongue should adequately recount His praise, or that human heart comprehend His fathomless mystery. He is, and hath every been, veiled in the ancient eternity of His Essence, and will remain in His Reality everlastingly hidden from the sight of men. 'No vision taketh in Him, but He taketh in all vision; He is the Subtle, the All-Perceiving.'

The door of the knowledge of the Ancient of Days being thus closed in the face of all beings, the Source of infinite grace, according to His saying, 'His grace hath transcended all things; My grace hath encompassed them all,' hath caused those luminous Gems of Holiness to appear out of the realm of the spirit, in the noble form of the human temple, and be made manifest unto all men, that they may impart unto the world the mysteries of the unchangeable Being, and tell of the subtleties of His imperishable Essence. These sanctified Mirrors, these Day Springs of ancient glory, are, one and all, the Exponents on earth of Him Who is the central Orb of the universe, its Essence and ultimate Purpose. From Him proceed their knowledge and power; from Him is derived their sovereignty. The beauty of their countenance is but a reflection of His image, and their revelation a sign of His deathless glory. They are the Treasuries of Divine knowledge, and the Repositories of celestial wisdom. Through them is transmitted a grace that is infinite, and by them is revealed the Light that can never fade. (*Kitáb-i-Iqán* 98-100)

These Tabernacles of Holiness, these Primal Mirrors which reflect the light of unfading glory, are but expressions of Him Who is the Invisible of the Invisible. By the revelation of these Gems of Divine virtue all the names and attributes of God, such as knowledge and power, sovereignty and dominion, mercy and wisdom, glory, bounty, and grace, are made manifest.

These attributes of God are not, and have never been, vouchsafed specially unto certain Prophets, and withheld from others. Nay, all the Prophets of God, His well-favoured, His holy and chosen Messengers are, without exception, the bearers of His names, and the embodiments of His attributes. They only differ in the intensity of their revelation, and the comparative potency of their light. Even as He hath revealed: 'Some of the Apostles We have caused to excel the others.' It hath, therefore, become manifest and evident that within the tabernacles of these Prophets and chosen Ones of God the light of His infinite names and exalted attributes hath been reflected, even though the light of some of these attributes may or may not be outwardly revealed from these luminous Temples to the eyes of men. That a certain attribute of God hath not been outwardly manifested by these Essences of Detachment doth in no wise imply that they who are the Day Springs of God's attributes and the Treasuries of His holy names did not actually possess it. Therefore, these illuminated Souls, these beauteous Countenances have, each and every one of them, been endowed with all the attributes of God, such as sovereignty, dominion, and the like, even though to outward seeming they be shorn of all earthly majesty. To every discerning eye this is evident and manifest; it requireth neither proof nor evidence. (*Kitáb-i-Iqán* 103-4)

Know thou of a certainty that the Unseen can in no wise incarnate His Essence and reveal it unto men. He is, and hath ever been, immensely exalted beyond all that can either be recounted or perceived. From His retreat of glory His voice is ever proclaiming: 'Verily, I am God; there is none other God besides Me, the All-Knowing, the All-Wise. I have manifested Myself unto men, and have sent down Him Who is the Day Spring of the signs of My Revelation. Through Him I have caused all creation to testify that there is none other God except Him, the Incomparable, the All-Informed, the All-Wise.' (*Gleanings* 49)

He Who is everlastingly hidden from the eyes of men can never be known except through His Manifestation, and His Manifestation can adduce no greater proof of the truth of His Mission than the proof of His own Person.

The door of the knowledge of the Ancient Being hath ever been, and will continue for ever to be, closed in the face of men. No man's understanding shall ever gain access unto His holy court. As a token of His mercy, however, and as a proof of His loving-kindness, He hath manifested unto men the Day Stars of His divine guidance, the Symbols of His divine unity, and hath ordained the knowledge of these sanctified Beings to be identical with the knowledge of His own Self. Whoso recognizeth them hath recognized God. Whoso hearkeneth to their call, hath hearkened to the Voice of God, and whoso testifieth to the truth of their Revelation, hath testified to the truth of God Himself. Whoso turneth away from them, hath turned away from God, and whoso disbelieveth in them, hath disbelieved in God. Every one of them is the Way of God that connecteth this world with the realms above, and the Standard of His Truth unto every one in the kingdoms of earth and heaven. They are the Manifestations of God amidst men, the evidences of His Truth, and the signs of His glory. (*Gleanings* 49-50)

Who is it that can claim to have attained the heights of His exalted Essence, and what mind can measure the depths of His unfathomable mystery? (*Gleanings* 60)

Praise be to God, the All-Possessing, the King of incomparable glory, a praise which is immeasurably above the understanding of all created things, and is exalted beyond the grasp of the minds of men. None else besides Him hath ever been able to sing adequately His praise, nor will any man succeed at any time in describing the full measure of His glory. Who is it that can claim to have attained the heights of His exalted Essence, and what mind can measure the depths of His unfathomable mystery? From each and every revelation emanating from the Source of His glory, holy and never-ending evidences of unimaginable splendour have appeared, and out of every manifestation of His invincible power oceans of eternal light have outpoured. How immensely exalted are the wondrous testimonies of His almighty sovereignty, a glimmer of which, if it but touched them, would utterly consume all that are in the heavens and in the earth! How indescribably lofty are the tokens of His consummate power, a single sign of which, however inconsiderable, must transcend the comprehension of whatsoever hath, from the beginning that hath no beginning, been brought into being, or will be created in the future till the end that hath no end. All the Embodiments of His Names wander in the wilderness of search, athirst and eager to discover His Essence, and all the Manifestations of His Attributes implore Him, from the Sinai of Holiness, to unravel His mystery.

    A drop of the billowing ocean of His endless mercy hath adorned all creation with the ornament of existence, and a breath wafted from His peerless Paradise hath invested all beings with the robe of His sanctity and glory. A sprinkling from the unfathomed deep of His sovereign and all-pervasive Will hath, out of utter nothingness, called into being a creation which is infinite in its range and deathless in its duration. The wonders of His bounty can never cease, and the stream of His merciful grace can never be arrested. The process of His creation hath had no beginning, and can have no end. (*Gleanings* 60-1)

✺

How all-encompassing are the wonders of His boundless grace! Behold how they have pervaded the whole of creation. Such is their virtue that not a single atom in the entire universe can be found which doth not declare the evidences of His might, which doth not glorify His holy Name, or is not expressive of the effulgent light of His unity. So perfect and comprehensive is His creation that no mind nor heart, however keen or pure, can ever grasp the nature of the most insignificant of His creatures; much less fathom the mystery of Him Who is the Day Star of Truth, Who is the invisible and unknowable Essence. The conceptions of the devoutest of mystics, the attainments of the most accomplished amongst men, the highest praise which human tongue or pen can render are all the product of man's finite mind and are conditioned by its limitations. (*Gleanings* 62)

✺

From time immemorial He hath been veiled in the ineffable sanctity of His exalted Self, and will everlastingly continue to be wrapt in the impenetrable mystery of His unknowable Essence. Every attempt to attain to an understanding of His inaccessible Reality hath ended in complete bewilderment, and every effort to approach His exalted Self and envisage His Essence hath resulted in hopelessness and failure.

How bewildering to me, insignificant as I am, is the attempt to fathom the sacred depths of Thy knowledge! How futile my efforts to visualize the magnitude of the power inherent in Thine handiwork - the revelation of Thy creative power! How can mine eye, which hath no faculty to perceive itself, claim to have discerned Thine Essence, and how can mine heart, already powerless to apprehend the significance of its own potentialities, pretend to have comprehended Thy nature? How can I claim to have known Thee, when the entire creation is bewildered by Thy mystery, and how can I confess not to have known Thee, when, lo, the whole universe proclaimeth Thy Presence and testifieth to Thy truth? The portals of Thy grace have throughout eternity been open, and the means of access unto Thy Presence made available, unto all created things, and the revelations of Thy matchless Beauty have at all times been imprinted upon the realities of all beings, visible and invisible. Yet, notwithstanding this most gracious favour, this perfect and consummate bestowal, I am moved to testify that Thy court of holiness and glory is immeasurably exalted above the knowledge of all else besides Thee, and the mystery of Thy Presence is inscrutable to every mind except Thine own. No one except Thyself can unravel the secret of Thy nature, and naught else but Thy transcendental Essence can grasp the reality of Thy unsearchable being.

How vast the number of those heavenly and all-glorious beings who, in the wilderness of their separation from Thee, have wandered all the days of their lives, and failed in the end to find Thee! How great the multitude of the sanctified and immortal souls who were lost and bewildered while seeking in the desert of search to behold Thy face! Myriad are Thine ardent lovers whom the consuming flame of remoteness from Thee hath caused to sink and perish, and numberless are the faithful souls who have willingly laid down their lives in the hope of gazing on the light of Thy countenance. The sighs and moans of these longing hearts that pant after Thee can never reach Thy holy court, neither can the lamentations of the wayfarers that thirst to appear before Thy face attain Thy seat of glory. (Gleanings 62-4)

If the things which have been created by Him - magnified be His glory - and ordained to be the manifestations of His names and attributes, stand, by virtue of the grace with which they have been endowed, exalted beyond all proximity and remoteness, how much loftier must be that Divine Essence that hath called them into being? (*Gleanings* 184-5)

He, in truth, hath, throughout eternity, been one in His Essence, one in His attributes, one in His works. Any and every comparison is applicable only to His creatures, and all conceptions of association are conceptions that belong solely to those that serve Him. Immeasurably exalted is His Essence above the descriptions of His creatures. He, alone, occupieth the Seat of transcendent majesty, of supreme and inaccessible glory. The birds of men's hearts, however high they soar, can never hope to attain the heights of His unknowable Essence. It is He Who hath called into being the whole of creation, Who hath caused every created thing to spring forth at His behest. Shall, then, the thing that was born by virtue of the word which His Pen hath revealed, and which the finger of His Will hath directed, be regarded as partner with Him, or an embodiment of His Self? Far be it from His glory that human pen or tongue should hint at His mystery, or that human heart conceive His Essence. All else besides Him stand poor and desolate at His door, all are powerless before the greatness of His might, all are but slaves in His Kingdom. He is rich enough to dispense with all creatures.

The tie of servitude established between the worshiper and the adored One, between the creature and the Creator, should in itself be regarded as a token of His gracious favour unto men, and not as an indication of any merit they may possess. To this testifieth every true and discerning believer. (*Gleanings* 193-4)

... that ideal King hath, throughout eternity, been in His Essence independent of the comprehension of all beings, and will continue, for ever, in His own Being to be exalted above the adoration of every soul. (*Kitáb-i-Iqán* 52-3)

✺

... know thou that We bear witness unto that whereunto God hath Himself borne witness ere the creation of the heavens and of the earth, that there is none other God but Him, the Almighty, the All-Bounteous. We testify that He is One in His Essence, One in His attributes. He hath none to equal Him in the whole universe, nor any partner in all creation. He hath sent forth His Messengers, and sent down His Books, that they may announce unto His creatures the Straight Path. (*Tablets of Bahá'u'lláh* 212)

WHAT IS
THE PURPOSE OF LIFE?

When we consider the question of life's purpose, we must take a step back and first consider what 'purpose' means. Usually it is understood in the context of function. If we can discover the function of an object, we can then identify its most likely purpose, but can we be clear about the function of human existence? What about the question of meaning? For many people, a life without purpose is a life without meaning. If a life does not have a purpose, is meaninglessness a possibility? Is it indeed possible to live without a purpose, or do human beings assume some form of conscious or unconscious purpose irrespective of belief in a higher or divine one? Is it possible to know with certainty whether life does or does not have either meaning or purpose?

In Bahá'u'lláh's writings there are many passages with a definite point of view on these issues. He regards spirituality as central to human reality and this underlying assumption places the issue of purpose in the context of humanity's ability to develop its inherent spiritual potential. This spiritual capacity determines man's most distinguishing function and the basis of human purpose.

The relationship between our spiritual potential and our purpose in life is like the relationship between the engine of a car and that car's purpose. We can use the car for storage but such a use does not adequately utilize its true potential which is transportation. In the same way, if we live in a purely materialistic way, we do not utilize our spiritual capacity. Since function is the key to purpose, our spiritual capacities clearly indicate that we have some purpose in life which is connected with spirituality.

In the earliest Hebrew Scriptures the purpose of life rested on the idea that humanity was 'created in the image of God'. Like the New Testament and the Qur'án, Bahá'u'lláh's writings reflect the symbolism of this ancient religious tradition, and He too refers to this statement in affirming the basic spiritual reality of humanity. However, he does not give it a literal meaning in the physical sense; instead He expresses it in mystical terms, writing:

> Veiled in My immemorial being and in the ancient eternity of My essence, I knew My love for thee; therefore I created thee, have engraved on thee Mine image and revealed to thee My beauty. (*Hidden Words*, Arabic no. 3)

The concept of 'the image of God' has for ages defined the essential reality of the human individual as one potentially possessing qualities attributable to God: rationality, knowledge, justice, creativity and so on. Thus the purpose of life, from a religious point of view, has always been expressed in terms of such spiritual capacities. From this purpose we can perceive meaning in life. Stated simply, the objective of our existence is to become *like* God, or as much like God as is possible within the limits of the relationship between the created and the Creator. We cannot become God.

It is perhaps worthwhile pondering the reason Scriptures never simply stated what is the purpose of life. Sacred texts generally abound in symbolic imagery rather than philosophical explanations. Rather than directly state the purpose of life so that individuals could consider how they might achieve it, the ancient texts set forth inducements often using symbols (for example, heaven, hell, release from reincarnation, etc.) that were intended to motivate people to live in such a way that their purpose was realized and achieved.

One use of such symbolism unfolds in the story of the Garden of Eden, where man is immortal and able to exist in a close relationship with God, even with 'God walking in the garden in the cool of the day' (*Genesis* 3:8). But creation is followed by man's disobedience, 'the fall from grace', the expulsion from Paradise, and entrance into the world of contingent reality with its concurrent mortality, pain and suffering. However, a divine plan is set forth, an agreement or covenant is established, by which man can be redeemed. Faithfulness to this covenant is rewarded by an eventual restoration of what is essentially the original Paradise. This restoration brings us to the 'end' which is described in the concluding pages of the Bible.

Thus, the text relates a sacred history which begins with paradise and ends with paradise. The key elements are the idea that a life unconstrained by the suffering of contingent existence is possible, for this was the original condition, and that this paradise can be restored through the practice of spiritual living. For example, in one passage it is written, 'To him that overcometh will I give to eat of the tree of life, which is in the midst of the Paradise of God' (*Revelation* 2:7). The fulfilment of the promise is dependant on the faithfulness of the believer. The development of spirituality, which is the true purpose of life, is therefore closely related to the attainment of Paradise itself. Human beings have an essentially spiritual reality which, if fulfilled, brings them to their goal. When a person is born this reality and potentiality is present, but as a person's life unfolds it is often forgotten or abandoned. Through the individual's spiritual response it is restored, and Paradise attained.

The spiritual message of this ancient symbolism is reflected in these words of Bahá'u'lláh:

> Have ye forgotten that true and radiant morn, when in those hallowed and blessed surroundings ye were all gathered in My presence beneath the shade of the tree of life, which is planted in the all-glorious paradise? Awe-struck ye listened as I gave utterance to these three most holy words: O friends! Prefer not your will to Mine, never desire that which I have not desired for you, and approach Me not with lifeless hearts, defiled with worldly desires and cravings. Would ye but sanctify your souls, ye would at this present hour recall that place and those surroundings, and the truth of My utterance should be made evident unto all of you. (*The Hidden Words*, Persian no. 19)

The biblical version of this vision is cast into a history, a linear time scale, progressing from the fall to an eventual restoration. Although elements of this vision suggest an historical chronology, the message is more individual than historical; historical elements metaphorically represent the potential steps in the life of every soul: original purity, temptation, fall, expulsion, repentance, belief and restoration. Today, many people have come to believe that the events portrayed in the Bible are not an objective depiction of literal history and some people have therefore rejected them as fiction. However, if we view the things described in these accounts as symbols which are not to be taken literally, the fact that they are not objective history does not prevent them from representing something that is very real and which is both attainable and substantiated through religious experience. For example, although 'heaven' and 'hell' are not literal places, one in the clouds, the other in a fiery underworld, what they signify - the happiness, grief or pain that result depending on how we live our lives - are, nevertheless, a reality. Whether the spirituality of our lives is motivated by a limited literal interpretation or a deeper appreciation of what the symbols of Scripture actually signify is not of primary importance.

In Bahá'u'lláh's writings symbolic language is still present. For example, He refers to the 'tree of divine knowledge', the 'river of everlasting life' and speaks of attaining 'the Paradise of God's remembrance' and 'the Paradise of the love of God', all symbolic expressions alluding to the imagery of ancient Scripture. But His message goes beyond the purely personal context of each individual seeker after God and also teaches that this path from the fall to paradise applies to the whole of humanity in a progressive historical sense. Its culmination is the achievement of a spiritual society living in what He refers to and prophesies as an inevitable 'Most Great Peace', the equivalent of the Kingdom of God on Earth as anticipated by various religious traditions in both the West and Far East.

Apart from this symbolic framework, which assists people to perceive both a purpose to their lives and find the motivation for realizing it, there are many instances where He addresses the question of 'purpose' more directly. The following passages provide a selection of such statements.

*Excerpts from
the
Writings of Bahá'u'lláh*

✲

Having created the world and all that liveth and moveth therein, He, through the direct operation of His unconstrained and sovereign Will, chose to confer upon man the unique distinction and capacity to know Him and to love Him - a capacity that must needs be regarded as the generating impulse and the primary purpose underlying the whole of creation. (*Gleanings* 65)

✲

The purpose of God in creating man hath been, and will ever be, to enable him to know his Creator and to attain His Presence. To this most excellent aim, this supreme objective, all the heavenly Books and the divinely-revealed and weighty Scriptures unequivocally bear witness. Whoso hath recognized the

Day Spring of Divine guidance and entered His holy court hath drawn nigh unto God and attained His Presence, a Presence which is the real Paradise, and of which the loftiest mansions of heaven are but a symbol. (*Gleanings* 70)

It is for this very purpose that in every age and dispensation the Prophets of God and His chosen Ones have appeared amongst men, and have evinced such power as is born of God and such might as only the Eternal can reveal. (*Gleanings* 68)

His purpose, however, is to enable the pure in spirit and the detached in heart to ascend, by virtue of their own innate powers, unto the shores of the Most Great Ocean, that thereby they who seek the Beauty of the All-Glorious may be distinguished and separated from the wayward and perverse. (*Gleanings* 71)

The Purpose of the one true God, exalted be His glory, in revealing Himself unto men is to lay bare those gems that lie hidden within the mine of their true and inmost selves. (*Gleanings* 287)

✺

The purpose of the one true God in manifesting Himself is to summon all mankind to truthfulness and sincerity, to piety and trustworthiness, to resignation and submissiveness to the Will of God, to forbearance and kindliness, to uprightness and wisdom. (*Gleanings* 299)

✺

Barter not the garden of eternal delight for the dust-heap of a mortal world. (*The Hidden Words, Persian* no. 39)

✺

We ask God, exalted be His glory, to confirm each one of the friends in that land in the acquisition of such praiseworthy characteristics as shall conduce to the spread of justice and equity among the peoples of the world. The first, the fundamental purpose underlying creation hath ever been, and will continue to be, none other than the appearance of trustworthiness and godliness, of sincerity and goodwill amongst mankind, for these qualities are the cause of peace, security and tranquillity. Blessed are those who possess such virtues. (*Trustworthiness* no. 7)

With the hands of loving-kindness I have planted in the holy garden of paradise the young tree of your love and friendship, and have watered it with the goodly showers of My tender grace; now that the hour of its fruiting is come, strive that it may be protected, and be not consumed with the flame of desire and passion. (*The Hidden Words*, Persian no. 34)

In the garden of thy heart plant naught but the rose of love, and from the nightingale of affection and desire loosen not thy hold. (*The Hidden Words*, Persian no. 3)

The instigators of this oppression are those very persons who, though so foolish, are reputed the wisest of the wise. Such is their blindness that, with unfeigned severity, they have cast into this fortified and afflictive Prison Him, for the servants of Whose Threshold the world hath been created. The Almighty, however, in spite of them and those that have repudiated the truth of this 'Great Announcement,' hath transformed this Prison House into the Most Exalted Paradise, the Heaven of Heavens. (*Gleanings* 116)

Thou hast gained admittance into the Paradise of God's Remembrance, through thy recognition of Him Who is the Embodiment of that Remembrance amongst men. (*Gleanings* 303)

The purport of these words is that whosoever in every dispensation is born of the Spirit and is quickened by the breath of the Manifestation of Holiness, he verily is of those that have attained unto 'life' and 'resurrection' and have entered into the 'paradise' of the love of God. (*Kitáb-i-Íqán* 118)

◎

These, indeed, are they whose wine is all that hath proceeded out of the mouth of Thy primal will, whose pure beverage is Thine enthralling call, whose heavenly River is Thy love, whose Paradise is entrance into Thy presence and reunion with Thee. (*Prayers and Meditations* 229)

WHY IS THERE SUFFERING AND EVIL IN THE WORLD?

One of the traditional arguments against the existence of God involves the question of evil and suffering. The argument goes something like this: If there is a God who is all good He would surely *want* to prevent evil, and if this same God is all-powerful, He would surely be *able* to prevent evil. Since evil exists, there cannot be a God who is both all good and all powerful.

The difficulties of accepting such an argument against the existence of a just, all-powerful God become apparent if we consider for a moment what a world without evil or suffering might be like. If there was no material need, there would equally be no sacrificial acts of generosity or compassion. If there were no life-threatening events there would be no opportunity for courage. In a world without errors, forgiveness has no meaning. Every spiritual quality comes into being and is developed through the struggle against some inequity, injustice or calamity. Tolstoy touched on one aspect of this truth in his novel *War and Peace* when Pierre Bezukhov concludes, 'If there were no suffering, man would not know his limitations, would not know himself' (481-2). It might be added, people would not overcome their limitations if there were no difficulties to challenge their abilities.

But could not God have created human beings already possessing every virtue and capacity in some fixed degree so that no improvement was required? Such a hypothetical alternative is difficult to imagine because acting virtuously seems inextricably linked to the freedom to do otherwise. Steadfastness, loyalty and detachment all seem to require temptation and the opportunity to choose for good or worse. In other words, virtues cease to be virtues without the freedoms that determine their existence. Does a person really possess courage who is never challenged, or honesty who is never tempted to deceive? In the words of Milton, 'I cannot praise a fugitive and cloistered virtue, unexercised and unbreathed, that never sallies out and sees her adversary' (*Areopagitia* 391). He adds, 'Wherefore did He create passions within us, pleasures round about us, but that these rightly tempered are the very ingredients of virtue?' (ibid. 395)

Suffering and evil are experienced in two ways: through the moral error of human beings, in dishonesty, violence, greed and so on, and through natural causes, in earthquakes, floods, droughts and diseases. Both suggest that pain and suffering are inseparable and woven into the contingencies of life. However, in both cases human beings can develop their spiritual potential through their response to these difficulties. The material world can never be more than a catalyst for the creation of paradise within our own selves and through our own efforts.

Our purpose is not to build a material paradise where we can lived hedonistically, having every desire fulfilled. Life in such a paradise would not be supportive of spiritual progress. As Bahá'u'lláh writes, 'Thou dost wish for gold and I desire thy freedom from it. Thou thinkest thyself rich in its possession, and I recognize thy wealth in thy sanctity therefrom' (*The Hidden Words*, Arabic no. 56). Bahá'u'lláh's focus on the soul and communion with God shifts the emphasis away from material existence as an end in itself, and in the process puts evil and suffering in the purposeful context of spiritual development.

Paradise is not a place without evil or the inherent pains and inequities of material existence, but a spiritual condition wherein such difficulties are continually being overcome by the higher potentialities of human beings. Rather than pursuing a life of pleasure we should seek a life of service. Hence Bahá'u'lláh writes, 'Strive not after bodily comforts, and keep your heart pure and stainless' (*Gleanings* 167-8). Devotion to God, according to Bahá'u'lláh's writings, is expressed in detachment and service, and developing a condition of selflessness. This is central to His persistent call to the spiritual life, 'Centre your thoughts in the Well-Beloved, rather than in your own selves' (*Gleanings* 167-8).

From this point of view, the difficulties and sufferings in the world are not inherently negative, rather the only real evil lies in the failure on the part of humanity to act spiritually. This failure consists in turning away from the path of God and pursuing one's own self-interest without regard for others. In one passage Bahá'u'lláh expressed this idea with these words, 'They say: "Where is Paradise, and where is Hell?" Say: "The one is reunion with Me; the other thine own self"' (*Epistle* 132).

When Bahá'u'lláh speaks of evil, therefore, it is not as a force in and of itself but as a lack of the presence of God. In one passage He writes, 'Be fair in your judgement. Every good thing is of God, and every evil thing is from yourselves' (*Gleanings* 149). He uses the familiar symbolism, found in ancient Scriptures, of Satan, the Evil One and Hell, but frequently hints at their symbolic meaning with such phrases as the 'Satan of self' (*Kitáb-i-Iqán* 112). In another passage He writes, 'Indeed the actions of man himself breed a profusion of satanic power. For were men to abide by and observe the divine teachings, every trace of evil would be banished from the face of the earth. However, the widespread differences that exist among mankind and the prevalence of sedition, contention, conflict and the like are the primary factors which provoke the appearance of the satanic spirit' (*Tablets of Bahá'u'lláh* 176-7).

Satan then does not refer to an independent and personal being but, rather, represents human nature when it is forgetful of or in opposition to the divine reality of God. As the character Ivan says in Dostoevsky's *The Brothers Karamazov*, 'I think if the devil doesn't exist, but that man has created him, he has created him in his own image and likeness' (123).

*Selections from
the
Writings of Bahá'u'lláh*

✪

Be generous in prosperity, and thankful in adversity. Be worthy of the trust of thy neighbour, and look upon him with a bright and friendly face. Be a treasure to the poor, an admonisher to the rich, an answerer of the cry of the needy, a preserver of the sanctity of thy pledge. Be fair in thy judgement, and guarded in thy speech. Be unjust to no man, and show all meekness to all men. Be as a lamp unto them that walk in darkness, a joy to the sorrowful, a sea for the thirsty, a haven for the distressed, an upholder and defender of the victim of oppression. Let integrity and uprightness distinguish all thine acts. Be a home for the stranger, a balm to the suffering, a tower of strength for the fugitive. Be eyes to the blind, and a guiding light unto the feet of the erring. Be an ornament to the countenance of truth, a crown to the brow of fidelity, a pillar of the temple of righteousness, a breath of life to the body of mankind, an ensign of the hosts of justice, a luminary above the horizon of virtue, a dew to the soil of the human heart, an ark on the ocean of knowledge, a sun in the heaven of bounty, a gem on the diadem of wisdom, a shining light in the firmament of thy generation, a fruit upon the tree of humility. (*Epistle* 93-4)

✺

O SON OF MAN! The true lover yearneth for tribulation even as doth the rebel for forgiveness and the sinful for mercy. (*The Hidden Words*, Arabic no. 49)

✺

O SON OF MAN! If adversity befall thee not in My path, how canst thou walk in the ways of them that are content with My pleasure? If trials afflict thee not in thy longing to meet Me, how wilt thou attain the light in thy love for My beauty? (*The Hidden Words*, Arabic no. 50)

✺

O SON OF MAN! My calamity is My providence, outwardly it is fire and vengeance, but inwardly it is light and mercy. Hasten thereunto that thou mayest become an eternal light and an immortal spirit. This is

My command unto thee, do thou observe it. (*The Hidden Words*, Arabic no. 51)

○

O SON OF MAN! Should prosperity befall thee, rejoice not, and should abasement come upon thee, grieve not, for both shall pass away and be no more. (*The Hidden Words*, Arabic no. 52)

○

O SON OF BEING! If poverty overtake thee, be not sad; for in time the Lord of wealth shall visit thee. Fear not abasement, for glory shall one day rest on thee. (*The Hidden Words*, Arabic no. 53)

○

He discerneth the truth in all things, through the guidance of Him Who is the All-Seeing. The civilization, so often vaunted by the learned exponents of arts and sciences, will, if allowed to overleap the bounds of moderation, bring great evil upon men. Thus warneth you He Who is the All-Knowing. If carried to excess, civilization will prove as prolific a source of evil as it had been of goodness when kept within the restraints of moderation. Meditate on this, O people, and be not of them that wander distraught in the wilderness of error. (*Gleanings* 342-3)

❊

O SON OF BEING! If thine heart be set upon this eternal, imperishable dominion, and this ancient, everlasting life, forsake this mortal and fleeting sovereignty. (*The Hidden Words*, Arabic no. 54)

❊

O SON OF MAN! For everything there is a sign. The sign of love is fortitude under My decree and patience under My trials. (*The Hidden Words*, Arabic no.48)

❊

The virtues and attributes pertaining unto God are all evident and manifest, and have been mentioned and described in all the heavenly Books. Among them are trustworthiness, truthfulness, purity of heart while communing with God, forbearance, resignation to whatever the Almighty hath decreed, contentment with the things His Will hath provided, patience, nay, thankfulness in the midst of tribulation, and complete reliance, in all circumstances, upon Him. These rank, according to the estimate of God, among the highest and most laudable of all acts. All other acts are, and will ever remain, secondary and subordinate unto them . . .

The spirit that animateth the human heart is the knowledge of God, and its truest adorning is the recognition of the truth that "He doeth whatsoever He willeth, and ordaineth that which He pleaseth." Its raiment is the fear of God, and its perfection steadfastness in His Faith. Thus God instructeth whosoever seeketh Him. He, verily, loveth the one that turneth towards Him. There is none other God but Him, the Forgiving, the Most Bountiful. All praise be to God, the Lord of all worlds. (*Gleanings* 290-1)

Glory to Thee, O my God! But for the tribulations which are sustained in Thy path, how could Thy true lovers be recognized; and were it not for the trials which are borne for love of Thee, how could the station of such as yearn for Thee be revealed? Thy might beareth me witness! The companions of all who adore Thee are the tears they shed, and the comforters of such as seek Thee are the groans they utter, and the food of them who haste to meet Thee is the fragments of their broken hearts.

How sweet to my taste is the bitterness of death suffered in Thy path, and how precious in my estimation are the shafts of Thine enemies when encountered for the sake of the exaltation of Thy word! Let me quaff in Thy Cause, O my God, whatsoever Thou didst desire, and send down upon me in Thy love all Thou didst ordain. By Thy glory! I wish only what Thou wishest, and cherish what Thou cherishest. In Thee have I, at all times, placed my whole trust and confidence. (*Epistle* 95)

❂

Glory to Thee, O my God! But for the tribulations which are sustained in Thy path, how could Thy true lovers be recognized; and were it not for the trials which are borne for love of Thee, how could the station of such as yearn for Thee be revealed? (*Epistle* 125)

❂

Hear no evil, and see no evil, abase not thyself, neither sigh and weep. Speak no evil, that thou mayest not hear it spoken unto thee, and magnify not the faults of others that thine own faults may not appear great; and wish not the abasement of anyone, that thine own abasement be not exposed. Live then the days of thy life, that are less than a fleeting moment, with thy mind stainless, thy heart unsullied, thy thoughts pure, and thy nature sanctified, so that, free and content, thou mayest put away this mortal frame, and repair unto the mystic paradise and abide in the eternal kingdom for evermore. (*The Hidden Words*, Arabic no. 44)

○

Ye are even as the bird which soareth, with the full force of its mighty wings and with complete and joyous confidence, through the immensity of the heavens, until, impelled to satisfy its hunger, it turneth longingly to the water and clay of the earth below it, and, having been entrapped in the mesh of its desire, findeth itself impotent to resume its flight to the realms whence it came. (*Gleanings* 327)

○

They who have been inebriated with the wine of Thy knowledge, these, verily, hasten to meet every manner of adversity in their longing to pass into Thy presence. (*Prayers and Meditations* 7)

○

From the exalted source, and out of the essence of His favour and bounty He hath entrusted every created thing with a sign of His knowledge, so that none of His creatures may be deprived of its share in expressing, each according to its capacity and rank, this knowledge. This sign is the mirror of His beauty in the world of creation. The greater the effort exerted for the refinement of this sublime and noble mirror, the more faithfully will it be made to reflect the glory of the names and attributes of God, and reveal the wonders of His signs and knowledge. Every created thing will be enabled (so great is this reflecting power) to reveal the potentialities of its preordained station, will recognize its capacity and limitations, and will testify to the truth that 'He, verily, is God; there is none other God besides Him . . .

There can be no doubt whatever that, in consequence of the efforts which every man may consciously exert and as a result of the exertion of his own spiritual faculties, this mirror can be so cleansed from the dross of earthly defilements and purged from satanic fancies as to be able to draw nigh unto the meads of eternal holiness and attain the courts of everlasting fellowship. (*Gleanings* 262-3.)

O God! The trials Thou sendest are a salve to the sores of all them who are devoted to Thy will; the remembrance of Thee is a healing medicine to the hearts of such as have drawn nigh unto Thy court; nearness to Thee is the true life of them who are Thy lovers; Thy presence is the ardent desire of such as yearn to behold

Thy face; remoteness from Thee is a torment to those that have acknowledged Thy oneness, and separation from Thee is death unto them that have recognized Thy truth! (*Prayers and Meditations* 59)

How long wilt thou soar in the realms of desire? Wings have I bestowed upon thee, that thou mayest fly to the realms of mystic holiness and not the regions of satanic fancy. (*The Hidden Words*, Persian no. 79)

Dissipate not the wealth of your precious lives in the pursuit of evil and corrupt affection, nor let your endeavours be spent in promoting your personal interest. Be generous in your days of plenty, and be patient in the hour of loss. (*Tablets of Bahá'u'lláh* 138)

IS THERE
LIFE AFTER DEATH?

Freud wrote that 'philosophers have declared that the intellectual enigma presented to primitive man by the picture of death was what forced him to reflection, and thus that it became the starting-point of all speculation' (*War and Death* 763). Although Freud went on to reject that the question of death was an intellectual starting-point for human reflection, he didn't doubt the power it has exerted on human life. Speculation has encompassed a variety of theories and beliefs. Some Christians and Moslems believe that the eternal life mentioned in ancient Scripture refers to the future reconstitution of our physical bodies when God establishes the Kingdom of God on earth. Some Hindus and Buddhists adhere to an equally literal interpretation of scriptural references to reincarnation. Without rejecting the immortality of the soul or the inspiration of past Scriptures, Bahá'u'lláh appears to dismiss both of these interpretations. In one passage He writes, 'By the terms "life" and "death", spoken of in the scriptures, is intended the life of faith and the death of unbelief' (*Kitáb-i-Íqán* 114). He regards the life to come not as an extension of our physical lives here, but as an existence 'as different from this world as this world is different from that of a child while still in the womb of its mother' (*Gleanings* 157).

Bahá'u'lláh's teachings are consistently God-centric, and eternal life, or simply life itself, is understood to exist only in relationship to the attainment of closeness to God. Closeness to God is true life in this world and the next. To be far from God is death both in this life and the next. With this understanding it is possible to view His references to a Heaven and Hell conceptually rather than literally. That is, the symbols that He used in His teachings to speak about life after death are not intended to be physical depictions of another world, but rather are intended to motivate people to do what will bring them closer to God. This has always been the method used in the Scriptures. For example, reincarnation and the imagery of Heaven and Hell, if interpreted literally, present different pictures of immortality. However, when understood conceptually, both systems or views teach the same thing: the soul is immortal, our lives in this world serve a purpose, consequences after this life will follow according to the merits of our actions in this world, and the ideal condition is achieved only through seeking God and remaining steadfast in our faith. Both systems share these essential points and present descriptions of future life which evoke in human beings a moral response intended to bring the individual closer to God. The future life is real but the symbols are not literal.

The happiness beyond is always linked to devotion to God. St Paul wrote, 'Eye hath not seen, nor ear heard, neither have entered into the heart of man, the things which God hath prepared for them that love

Him' (*1 Corinthians* 2:9). Krishna assured Arjuna in the ancient Scriptures of the *Bhagavad-Gítá*, 'One can understand the Supreme Personality as He is only by devotional service. And when one is in full consciousness of the Supreme Lord by such devotion, he can enter into the kingdom of God. Though engaged in all kinds of activities, My devotee, under My protection, reaches the eternal and imperishable abode by My grace' (18:55-6). Such promises as these cannot but help motivate and inspire the believer.

In a number of passages Bahá'u'lláh affirms the belief in immortality, but He says 'the nature of the soul after death can never be described'. Addressing those who appeal to reason to 'deny the mysteries of life beyond', He points to the limitations of reason asking whether the spider can 'snare a phoenix in his web?'(*Seven Valleys* 33). The soul is, in His words, 'a heavenly gem whose reality the most learned of men hath failed to grasp, and whose mystery no mind, however acute, can ever hope to unravel' (*Gleanings* 158-9).

The nature of the soul and the life beyond are elusive, and exploring the subject on a philosophical or intellectual level is to some degree futile. Nevertheless, Bahá'u'lláh clearly wishes to assure those who have questioned Him of the reality of such an existence. To provide some ground for accepting His assertions He offers several arguments, both theological and empirical. As subjects in themselves, He only dwells upon them briefly.

Bahá'u'lláh's theological explanation points out the requirements of divine justice. That is, immortality and a future life rest upon belief in a just God who rewards and punishes His servants according to their faith, capacities and efforts. This belief tends to conjure up the depictions of a lush material Paradise and the fiery Hell of Dante's *Divine Comedy* . In Bahá'u'lláh's writings such imagery indicates no more than the symbols representative of God's eternal justice.

The belief in such future judgement has had a powerful influence on the way people have chosen to conduct their lives. This has led many to argue that the imagery in past Scriptures, such as the Qur'án, appealed to our baser material pleasures and fears to evoke obedience to more noble aspirations, and as such the entire concept of immortality is only valid as a means of instruction. Some even argue that immortality can be no more than an enduring memory or influence, even as Melville suggests, 'immortality is but ubiquity in time' (*Moby Dick* ch. 41).

However much this might appeal to our scepticism, Bahá'u'lláh's writings do not allow us to reduce 'immortality' to any entirely conceptual phenomena, such as memory or enduring influence. In several instances He refers to the empirical evidence of the individual body as an argument in favour of immortality. The body of the individual cannot be regarded as the true self or reality of the person. The existence of our consciousness or our rational faculty does not depend on any of the senses. Rather we use our senses as the driver of a car whose consciousness is wholly independent of it. The driver can leave the car without fear of extinction.

Bahá'u'lláh also points out the soul's independence

from the physical body by calling our attention to the soul's activities in the realm of dreams and the experience of *déjà vu*. His purpose is to show that the soul has a life apart from physical existence. Finally, He appeals to the sacrificial testimony of the Prophets: 'Wert thou to ponder in thine heart the behaviour of the Prophets of God thou wouldst assuredly and readily testify that there must needs be other worlds besides this world.' He adds, 'How could such Souls have consented to surrender themselves unto their enemies if they believed all the worlds of God to have been reduced to this earthly life?'

*Selections from
the
Writings of Bahá'u'lláh*

And now concerning thy question regarding the soul of man and its survival after death. Know thou of a truth that the soul, after its separation from the body, will continue to progress until it attaineth the presence of God, in a state and condition which neither the revolution of ages and centuries, nor the changes and chances of this world, can alter. It will endure as long as the Kingdom of God, His sovereignty, His dominion and power will endure. It will manifest the signs of God, and His attributes, and will reveal His loving kindness and bounty. The movement of My Pen is stilled when it attempteth to befittingly describe the loftiness and glory of so exalted a station. The honour with which the Hand of Mercy will invest the soul is such as no tongue can adequately reveal, nor any other earthly agency describe. Blessed is the soul which, at the hour of its separation from the body, is sanctified from the vain imaginings of the peoples of the world.

Such a soul liveth and moveth in accordance with the Will of its Creator, and entereth the all-highest Paradise. The Maids of Heaven, inmates of the loftiest mansions, will circle around it, and the Prophets of God and His chosen ones will seek its companionship. With them that soul will freely converse, and will recount unto them that which it hath been made to endure in the path of God, the Lord of all worlds. If any man be told that which hath been ordained for such a soul in the worlds of God, the Lord of the throne on high and of earth below, his whole being will instantly blaze out in his great longing to attain that most exalted, that sanctified and resplendent station. The nature of the soul after death can never be described, nor is it meet and permissible to reveal its whole character to the eyes of men. The Prophets and Messengers of God have been sent down for the sole purpose of guiding mankind to the straight Path of Truth. The purpose underlying their revelation hath been to educate all men, that they may, at the hour of death, ascend, in the utmost purity and sanctity and with absolute detachment, to the throne of the Most High. The light which these souls radiate is responsible for the progress of the world and the advancement of its peoples. They are like unto leaven which leaveneth the world of being, and constitute the animating force through which the arts and wonders of the world are made manifest. Through them the clouds rain their bounty upon men, and the earth bringeth forth its fruits. All things must have a cause, a motive power, an animating principle. These souls and symbols of detachment have provided, and will continue to provide, the supreme moving impulse in the world of being. The world beyond is as different from this world as this world is different from that of the child while still in the womb of its mother. When the soul attaineth the Presence of God, it will assume the form that best befitteth its immortality and is worthy of its celestial habitation. Such an existence is a contingent and not an absolute existence, inasmuch as the former is preceded by a cause, whilst the latter is independent thereof. Absolute existence is strictly confined to God, exalted be His glory. Well is it with them that apprehend this truth. Wert thou to ponder in thine heart the behaviour of the Prophets of God thou wouldst assuredly and readily testify that there must needs be other worlds besides this world. The majority of the truly wise and learned have, throughout the ages, as it hath been recorded by the Pen of Glory in the Tablet of Wisdom, borne witness to the truth of that which the holy Writ of God hath revealed. Even the materialists have testified in their writings to the wisdom of these divinely-appointed Messengers, and have regarded the references made by the Prophets to Paradise, to hell fire, to future reward and punishment, to have been actuated by a desire to educate and uplift the souls of men. Consider, therefore, how the generality of mankind, whatever their beliefs or theories, have recognized the excellence, and admitted the superiority, of these Prophets of God. These Gems of Detachment are acclaimed by some as the embodiments of wisdom, while others believe them to be the mouthpiece of God Himself. How could such

Souls have consented to surrender themselves unto their enemies if they believed all the worlds of God to have been reduced to this earthly life? Would they have willingly suffered such afflictions and torments as no man hath ever experienced or witnessed? (*Gleanings* 157-8)

✦

Thou hast asked Me concerning the nature of the soul. Know, verily, that the soul is a sign of God, a heavenly gem whose reality the most learned of men hath failed to grasp, and whose mystery no mind, however acute, can ever hope to unravel. It is the first among all created things to declare the excellence of its Creator, the first to recognize His glory, to cleave to His truth, and to bow down in adoration before Him. If it be faithful to God, it will reflect His light, and will, eventually, return unto Him. If it fail, however, in its allegiance to its Creator, it will become a victim to self and passion, and will, in the end, sink in their depths...

Much hath been written in the books of old concerning the various stages in the development of the soul, such as concupiscence, irascibility, inspiration, benevolence, contentment, Divine good-pleasure, and the like; the Pen of the Most High, however, is disinclined to dwell upon them. Every soul that walketh humbly with its God, in this Day, and cleaveth unto Him, shall find itself invested with the honour and glory of all goodly names and stations. When man is asleep, his soul can, in no wise, be said to have been inherently affected by any external object. It is not susceptible of any change in its original state or character. Any variation in its functions is to be ascribed to external causes. It is to these external influences that any variations in its environment, its understanding, and perception should be attributed. Consider the human eye. Though it hath the faculty of perceiving all created things, yet the slightest impediment may so obstruct its vision as to deprive it of the power of discerning any object whatsoever. Magnified be the name of Him Who hath created, and is the Cause of, these causes, Who hath ordained that every change and variation in the world of being be made dependent upon them. Every created thing in the whole universe is but a door leading into His knowledge, a sign of His sovereignty, a revelation of His names, a symbol of His majesty, a token of His power, a means of admittance into His straight Path . . .

Verily I say, the human soul is, in its essence, one of the signs of God, a mystery among His mysteries. It is one of the mighty signs of the Almighty, the harbinger that proclaimeth the reality of all the worlds of God. Within it lieth concealed that which the world is now utterly incapable of apprehending. Ponder in thine heart the revelation of the Soul of God that pervadeth all His Laws, and contrast it with that base and appetitive nature that hath rebelled against Him, that forbiddeth men to turn unto the Lord of Names, and impelleth them to walk after their lusts and wickedness.

Such a soul hath, in truth, wandered far in the path of error...

Thou hast, moreover, asked Me concerning the state of the soul after its separation from the body. Know thou, of a truth, that if the soul of man hath walked in the ways of God, it will, assuredly, return and be gathered to the glory of the Beloved. By the righteousness of God! It shall attain a station such as no pen can depict, or tongue describe. The soul that hath remained faithful to the Cause of God, and stood unwaveringly firm in His Path shall, after his ascension, be possessed of such power that all the worlds which the Almighty hath created can benefit through him. Such a soul provideth, at the bidding of the Ideal King and Divine Educator, the pure leaven that leaveneth the world of being, and furnisheth the power through which the arts and wonders of the world are made manifest. Consider how meal needeth leaven to be leavened with. Those souls that are the symbols of detachment are the leaven of the world. Meditate on this, and be of the thankful. In several of Our Tablets We have referred to this theme, and have set forth the various stages in the development of the soul. Verily I say, the human soul is exalted above all egress and regress. It is still, and yet it soareth; it moveth, and yet it is still. It is, in itself, a testimony that beareth witness to the existence of a world that is contingent, as well as to the reality of a world that hath neither beginning nor end. Behold how the dream thou hast dreamed is, after the lapse of many years, re-enacted before thine eyes. Consider how strange is the mystery of the world that appeareth to thee in thy dream. Ponder in thine heart upon the unsearchable wisdom of God, and meditate on its manifold revelations. (*Gleanings* 158-62)

❂

O SON OF THE SUPREME! I have made death a messenger of joy to thee. Wherefore dost thou grieve? I made the light to shed on thee its splendour. Why dost thou veil thyself therefrom? (*The Hidden Words*, Arabic no. 32)

❂

O SON OF MAN! The light hath shone on thee from the horizon of the sacred Mount and the spirit of enlightenment hath breathed in the Sinai of thy heart. Wherefore, free thyself from the veils of idle fancies and enter into My court, that thou mayest be fit for everlasting life and worthy to meet Me. Thus may death not come upon thee, neither weariness nor trouble. (*The Hidden Words*, Arabic no. 63)

❂

O SON OF BEING! Bring thyself to account each day ere thou art summoned to a reckoning; for death, unheralded, shall come upon thee and thou shalt be called to give account for thy deeds. (*The Hidden Words*, Arabic no. 33)

○

O SON OF SPIRIT! With the joyful tidings of light I hail thee: rejoice! To the court of holiness I summon thee; abide therein that thou mayest live in peace for evermore. (*The Hidden Words*, Arabic no. 33)

○

O SON OF SPIRIT! The spirit of holiness beareth unto thee the joyful tidings of reunion; wherefore dost thou grieve? The spirit of power confirmeth thee in His cause; why dost thou veil thyself? The light of His countenance doth lead thee; how canst thou go astray? (*The Hidden Words*, Arabic no. 34)

○

Consider the rational faculty with which God hath endowed the essence of man. Examine thine own self, and behold how thy motion and stillness, thy will and purpose, thy sight and hearing, thy sense of smell and power of speech, and whatever else is related to, or transcendeth, thy physical senses or spiritual perceptions, all proceed from, and owe their existence to, this same faculty. So closely are they related unto it, that if in less than the twinkling of an eye its relationship to the human body be severed, each and every one of these senses will cease immediately to exercise its function, and will be deprived of the power to manifest the evidences of its activity. It is indubitably clear and evident that each of these afore-mentioned instruments has depended, and will ever continue to depend, for its proper functioning on this rational faculty, which should be regarded as a sign of the revelation of Him Who is the sovereign Lord of all. Through its manifestation all these names and attributes have been revealed, and by the suspension of its action they are all destroyed and perish. It would be wholly untrue to maintain that this faculty is the same as the power of vision, inasmuch as the power of vision is derived from it and acteth in dependence upon it. It would, likewise, be idle to contend that this faculty can be identified with the sense of hearing, as the sense of hearing receiveth from the rational faculty the requisite energy for performing its functions. This same relationship bindeth this faculty with whatsoever hath been the recipient of these names and attributes within the human temple. These diverse names and revealed attributes have been generated through the agency of this sign of God. Immeasurably exalted is this sign, in its essence and reality, above all such names and attributes. Nay, all else besides it will, when compared with its glory, fade into utter nothingness and become a thing forgotten. Wert thou to ponder in thine heart, from now until the end that hath no end, and with all the concentrated intelligence and understanding which the greatest minds have attained in the past or will attain in the future, this divinely ordained and subtle Reality, this sign of the revelation of the All-Abiding, All-Glorious God, thou wilt fail to comprehend its mystery or to appraise its virtue. (*Gleanings* 155-65)

O SON OF JUSTICE! Whither can a lover go but to the land of his beloved? and what seeker findeth rest away from his heart's desire? To the true lover reunion is life, and separation is death. His breast is void of patience and his heart hath no peace. A myriad lives he would forsake to hasten to the abode of his beloved. (*The Hidden Words*, Persian no. 4)

With all his heart should the seeker avoid fellowship with evil doers, and pray for the remission of their sins. He should forgive the sinful, and never despise his low estate, for none knoweth what his own end shall be. How often hath a sinner, at the hour of death, attained to the essence of faith, and, quaffing the immortal draught, hath taken his flight unto the celestial Concourse. And how often hath a devout believer, at the hour of his soul's ascension, been so changed as to fall into the nethermost fire. Our purpose in revealing these convincing and weighty utterances is to impress upon the seeker that he should regard all else beside God as transient, and count all things save Him, Who is the Object of all adoration, as utter nothingness. (*Kitáb-i-Iqán* 194-5)

✧

O SON OF JUSTICE! Whither can a lover go but to the land of his beloved? and what seeker findeth rest away from his heart's desire? To the true lover reunion is life, and separation is death. His breast is void of patience and his heart hath no peace. A myriad lives he would forsake to hasten to the abode of his beloved. (*The Hidden Words*, Persian no. 4)

✧

. . . two of the people of Kúfih went to 'Ali, the Commander of the Faithful. One owned a house and wished to sell it; the other was to be the purchaser. They had agreed that this transaction should be effected and the contract be written with the knowledge of 'Ali. He, the exponent of the law of God, addressing the scribe, said: 'Write thou: "A dead man hath bought from another dead man a house. That house is bounded by four limits. One extendeth toward the tomb, the other to the vault of the grave, the third to the Sirát, the fourth to either Paradise or hell." ' Reflect, had these two souls been quickened by the trumpet-call of 'Ali, had they risen from the grave of error by the power of his love, the judgement of death would certainly not have been pronounced against them.

In every age and century, the purpose of the Prophets of God and their chosen ones hath been no other but to affirm the spiritual significance of the terms 'life', 'resurrection', and 'judgement'. If one will ponder but for a while this utterance of 'Ali in his heart, one will surely discover all mysteries hidden in the terms 'grave', 'tomb', 'sirát', 'paradise' and 'hell'. But oh! how strange and pitiful! Behold, all the people are imprisoned within the tomb of self, and lie buried beneath the nethermost depths of worldly desire! Wert thou to attain to but a dewdrop of the crystal waters of divine knowledge, thou wouldst readily realize that true life is not the life of the flesh but the life of the spirit. For the life of the flesh is common to both men and animals, whereas the life of the spirit is possessed only by the pure in heart who have quaffed from the ocean of faith and partaken of the fruit of certitude. This life knoweth no death, and this

*That is, 'The Valley of Wonderment'. This is one of the mystical valleys described in Bahá'u'lláh's work *The Seven Valleys* through which the seeker travels in search of God.

existence is crowned by immortality. Even as it hath been said: 'He who is a true believer liveth both in this world and in the world to come.' If by 'life' be meant this earthly life, it is evident that death must needs overtake it. (*Kitáb-i-Iqán* 119-21)

Indeed, O Brother, if we ponder each created thing, we shall witness a myriad perfect wisdoms and learn a myriad new and wondrous truths. One of the created phenomena is the dream. Behold how many secrets are deposited therein, how many wisdoms treasured up, how many worlds concealed. Observe, how thou art asleep in a dwelling, and its doors are barred; on a sudden thou findest thyself in a far-off city, which thou enterest without moving thy feet or wearying thy body; without using thine eyes, thou seest; without taxing thine ears, thou hearest; without a tongue, thou speakest. And perchance when ten years are gone, thou wilt witness in the outer world the very things thou hast dreamed tonight.

Now there are many wisdoms to ponder in the dream, which none but the people of this Valley* can comprehend in their true elements. First, what is this world, where without eye and ear and hand and tongue a man puts all of these to use? Second, how is it that in the outer world thou seest today the effect of a dream, when thou didst vision it in the world of sleep some ten years past? Consider the difference between these two worlds and the mysteries which they conceal, that thou mayest attain to divine confirmations and heavenly discoveries and enter the regions of holiness.

God, the Exalted, hath placed these signs in men, to the end that philosophers may not deny the mysteries of the life beyond nor belittle that which hath been promised them. For some hold to reason and deny whatever the reason comprehendeth not, and yet weak minds can never grasp the matters which we have related, but only the Supreme, Divine Intelligence can comprehend them: How can feeble reason encompass the Qur'án, or the spider snare a phoenix in his web? (*The Seven Valleys* 32-3)

◎

As to Paradise: It is a reality and there can be no doubt about it, and now in this world it is realized through love of Me and My good-pleasure. Whosoever attaineth unto it God will aid him in this world below, and after death He will enable him to gain admittance into Paradise whose vastness is as that of heaven and earth. Therein the Maids of glory and holiness will wait upon him in the daytime and in the night season, while the day-star of the unfading beauty of his Lord will at all times shed its radiance upon him and he will shine so brightly that no one shall bear to gaze at him. Such is the dispensation of Providence, yet the people are shut out by a grievous veil.

Likewise apprehend thou the nature of hell-fire and be of them that truly believe. For every act performed there shall be a recompense according to the estimate of God, and unto this the very ordinances and prohibitions prescribed by the Almighty amply bear witness. For surely if deeds were not rewarded and yielded no fruit, then the Cause of God - exalted is He - would prove futile. Immeasurably high is He exalted above such blasphemies! However, unto them that are rid of all attachments a deed is, verily, its own reward. Were We to enlarge upon this theme numerous Tablets would need to be written. (*Tablets of Bahá'u'lláh* 189)

CONCLUSION

In Dostoevsky's *The Brothers Karamazov*, a society lady confesses to a monk that 'the thought of the life beyond the grave distracts me to anguish, to terror'. She then appeals to him, asking how she can 'prove' what will bring her back to her faith. He tells her, 'there's no proving it, though you can be convinced of it'. When she asks how, he replies, 'By the experience of active love. Strive to love your neighbour actively and indefatigably. In as far as you advance in love you will grow surer of the reality of God and of the immortality of your soul. If you attain to perfect self-forgetfulness in the love of your neighbour, then you will believe without doubt, and no doubt can possibly enter your soul. This has been tried. This is certain' (*op. cit.* 26).

By suggesting what can be tried and proven to support what is beyond knowing, the monk steps beyond intellectual limitations. Living with mystery comes to enrich one's life, rather than trouble it.

As a response to mystery, the religious experience is an act of immersion, a baptism into age-old questions and answers that lie beneath the surface of our material existence. Many people have argued, perhaps more in the past than today, that if we open the religious books of former times we will find the answers to the basic questions that have intrigued and troubled the human mind since the beginning of known history. But these answers are themselves, while sometimes seemingly straight-forward, more ethereal and abstruse than some are ready to admit. Did God create the world in seven days? Are there flowing streams of pure water in heaven? Yes, say many of the world's Scriptures. But the Scriptures are full of symbols and we are compelled by reflection to accept that the spiritual reality is something that lies beneath what the sacred imagery depicts.

Our interpretation of explanations or answers is an important part of our search, and is greatly affected by our state of mind. This is especially important to consider when examining the religious and mystical writings of the Prophets, apostles and spiritual adepts. If we are impatient in our quest we may hastily confuse symbols with the reality they seek to explain, leading us to reject what seems improbable or too readily accept without understanding. Or we can, of course, simply end the search by refusing to acknowledge that there are symbols in such writings. It all depends on the extent to which we are willing to explore the issues.

Scripture is not immune to questions, and once we have asked, 'Is there a purpose in the answers that are given, and might not that purpose affect the nature of how the answers are expressed?', then the answers appear less literal and concrete. The seeming 'answers' given by the Prophets and sages may not be the point at all. In the end we may discover that it is not the answers that matter but the response these answers evoke in us and how they affect the way we live in relationship to mystery. As Bahá'u'lláh writes, 'Having recognized thy powerlessness to attain to an adequate understanding of that Reality which abideth within thee, thou wilt readily admit the futility of such efforts as may be attempted by thee, or by any of the created things, to fathom the mystery of the Living God, the Day Star of unfading glory, the Ancient of everlasting days. This confession of helplessness which mature contemplation must eventually impel every mind to make is in itself the acme of human understanding, and marketh the culmination of man's development' (*Gleanings* 155-66).

SELECTED BIBLIOGRAPHY OF WORKS BY BAHA'U'LLAH

Epistle to the Son of the Wolf. Trans. Shoghi Effendi. Wilmette, Ill.: Bahá'í Publishing Trust, 1941, 3rd rev. edn., 1976.

Gleanings from the Writings of Bahá'u'lláh. Trans. Shoghi Effendi. Wilmette, Ill.: Bahá'í Publishing Trust, 1939, 2nd edn., 1956.

The Hidden Words of Bahá'u'lláh. Trans. Shoghi Effendi. Wilmette, Ill.: Bahá'í Publishing Trust, 1939: London: Oneworld Publications, 1986.

The Kitáb-i-Iqán. Trans. Shoghi Effendi. Wilmette, Ill.: Bahá'í Publishing Trust, 1931, 3rd edn., 1974.

Prayers and Meditations by Bahá'u'lláh. Comp. and trans. Shoghi Effendi. London: Bahá'í Publishing Trust, 1957, 1978.

The Seven Valleys and The Four Valleys of Bahá'u'lláh. Trans. Marzieh Gail. Wilmette, Ill.: Bahá'í Publishing Trust, 1945, 1978.

Tablets of Bahá'u'lláh Revealed After the Kitáb-i-Aqdas. Comp. Research Department of the Universal House of Justice, trans. Habib Taherzadeh and a Committee at the Bahá'í World Centre. Haifa, Israel: Bahá'í World Centre, 1978.

ONEWORLD PUBLICATIONS

Accents of God
A TREASURY OF THE WORLD'S SACRED SCRIPTURES
M.K. Rohani

Presents six profound selections of major significance from the sacred writings of Hinduism, Judaism, Buddhism, Christianity, Islam and the Bahá'í Faith. The passages chosen for this special anthology highlight the common basis of mankind's spiritual heritage, and explore the eternal truths enshrined in these traditions. Beautifully produced with illustrations, this book is an attractive, large format gift edition.
86 pages, hardcover, £10.95, US$18.95

Achieving Peace by the Year 2000
by John Huddleston

In this insightful analysis of the causes of war and barriers to peace, the Chief of Budget & Planning at the IMF examines the psychological, moral and practical issues and puts forward a twelve point plan for establishing a lasting peace.
160 pages, softcover, £3.50, US$5.95

Drawings, Verse & Belief
by Bernard Leach

This beautiful, cloth-bound gift edition combines the author-artist's delicate visual images, spiritual reflections and delightful verse to provide a rare insight into the personality of a great master craftsman.
160 pages, 82 illustrations, cloth, £12.95, US$19.95

The Hidden Words of Bahá'u'lláh

An unusual and inspiring collection of spiritual teachings which will appeal to people of all religious persuasions and those who seek a spiritual life. Lucid in style and rich in imagery, these exquisite meditational verses explore the relationship between God and man.
112 pages, softcover, £3.95, US$6.95

ORDER FORM

Name _____

Address _____

_____

_____ Date _____

Quantity	Title	Price	Total
	To Understand & Be Understood	(s/c) £4.50/US$7.50	
	The Way to Inner Freedom	(s/c) £4.50/US$7.50	
	Creating a Successful Family	(h/c) £10.50/US$18.95	
	Accents of God	(s/c) £6.95/US$12.95	
	The Inner Limits of Mankind	(h/c) £8.95/US$14.95	
	Achieving Peace by the Year 2000	(s/c) £3.50/US$5.95	
	The Promise of World Peace	(s/c) £8.95/US$14.95	
	The Prophecies of Jesus	(s/c) £10.95/$18.95	
	A Study of Bahá'u'lláh's Tablet to the Christians	(h/c) £12.95/US $22.95	
		(s/c) £7.95/US$13.95	
	The Hidden Words of Bahá'u'lláh	(h/c) £8.95/US$13.95	
		(s/c) £3.95/US$6.95	
	Contemplating Life's Greatest Questions	(s/c) £4.50/US$7.95	
	Valley of Search	(s/c) £6.95/US$11.95	
	One People One Planet	(s/c) £7.95/US$13.95	
	Science & Religion	(s/c) £4.50/US$7.50	
	Drawings, Verse & Beliefs	(h/c) £12.95/US$19.95	

Please add 15% to all orders (min. £1/US$2)
Payment should accompany all orders.

Sub Total	
Postage & Handling	
Total	

Payment by: ____ Cheque/Money Order ____ Mastercard/Access ____ Visa

Exp. Date _____

Credit Card No. |_|_|_|_|_|_|_|_|_|_|_|_|_|_|_|_|

Signature _____

Send all orders to: Oneworld Publications
185 Banbury Road
Oxford, England OX2 7AR